DEC 2016

P9-CLR-343

MARY BOWSER AND THE
CIVIL WAR
SPY RING

Spy on History

MARY BOWSER AND THE CIVIL WAR SPY RING

Written by Enigma Alberti
Illustrated by Tony Cliff

Workman Publishing
New York

BRITISH TER

WASHINGTON TERRITORY

DAKOTA TERRITORY

OREGON

NEBRASKA TERRITORY

NEVADA TERRITORY

UTAH TERRITORY

COLORADO TERRITORY

KAN

CALIFORNIA

ARIZONA TERRITORY

NEW MEXICO TERRITORY

T

T

MEXICO

STATES AND TERRITORIES
OF THE UNITED STATES, 1863

Scale in miles

100 50 0   100   200   300

MAINE

VERMONT

NEW
HAMP-
SHIRE

MASSACHUSETTS

CON-
NECTICUT

RHODE ISLAND

MICHIGAN

NEW YORK

WISCONSIN

NEW JERSEY

PENNSYLVANIA

DELAWARE

OTA

IOWA

OHIO

MARYLAND

DIST. OF
COLUMBIA

ILLINOIS

INDIANA

WEST
VIRGINIA

VIRGINIA

KENTUCKY

MISSOURI

NORTH CAROLINA

TENNESSEE

SOUTH
CAROLINA

ARKANSAS

MISSISSIPPI

ALABAMA

GEORGIA

RY

LOUISIANA

FLORIDA

Union Free States & Territories ....

Union Slave-Holding States ....

Confederate States ....

Copyright © 2016 by Workman Publishing Co., Inc.
Text by Enigma Alberti
Illustrations by Tony Cliff

Library of Congress Cataloging-in-Publication Data is available.

ISBN 978-0-7611-8739-4

Designer: Colleen AF Venable
Editor: Daniel Nayeri
Production editor: Amanda Hong
Production manager: Julie Primavera

Workman books are available at special discounts when purchased in bulk for premiums and sales promotions as well as for fund-raising or educational use. Special editions or book excerpts can also be created to specification. For details, contact the Special Sales Director at the address below, or send an email to specialmarkets@workman.com.

Workman Publishing Co., Inc.
225 Varick Street
New York, NY 10014-4381

workman.com

WORKMAN is a registered trademark of Workman Publishing Co., Inc.

Printed in China
First printing February 2017

10 9 8 7 6 5 4 3 2 1

This book is a mystery story.

But there's also a mystery *in the book itself.*

At the end of the story, you'll find a letter from Mary.

Use the clues in this envelope to decode other clues and codes you'll find through-out the book . . .

and discover Mary's last secret!

Inside the president's private office, Mary cracked the door and listened, to make sure the hallway was empty before she slipped out.

She could hear the other slaves and servants talking in the back garden. She could hear the pounding feet of President Davis's children as they chased each other through the rooms downstairs.

But the hall
was
silent.

Still, Mary hesitated in the dim light of the president's office, surrounded by his walls and walls of books, his imposing desk looming behind her.

She wasn't afraid.

Not exactly.

But she had only taken the job as a maid at the Confederate White House a few weeks before. So far, nobody had seemed to pay much notice to her. And that was just how Mary wanted it.

If nobody paid much attention to her, maybe nobody would realize that she wasn't half-witted, as she pretended to be.

Or that she wasn't even really a maid.

And the last thing she wanted was for someone to notice her sneaking out of President Davis's office.

But she couldn't stay there forever.

And after listening for several minutes, she still hadn't heard a sound.

So she pulled the door wide, and stepped into the hall.

As she did,

a H E A V Y hand

F E L L

on her

S H O U L D E R .

Mary whirled around, her heart pounding.

O'Melia, Mrs. Davis's Irish maid, stood before her, arms crossed over her broad chest. Her reddish face was twisted in a suspicious scowl.

Of all the servants who could have surprised Mary, O'Melia was the worst. Many of the servants and slaves had been kind to Mary since she arrived at the Davis residence a few weeks before.

But O'Melia had regarded Mary with nothing but distrust. Maybe O'Melia didn't like any other servant who might challenge her position as Mrs. Davis's favorite. Or maybe she just flat out didn't like Mary.

But Mary knew for a fact that there was no one in the president's house who could be more dangerous to her. O'Melia was very close to Mrs. Davis. She was so close to Mrs. Davis that O'Melia's suspicions could get Mary fired—or worse.

And Mary also knew that she hadn't heard a sound before she stepped out into the hall.

She quickly calculated that O'Melia must have been lying in wait.

"What are you doing here?" O'Melia demanded. "Where do you think you're going?"

Instantly, Mary shifted into the act that she'd been playing ever since she arrived at the Davis mansion: slow to understand but eager to please. She let her gaze fall to the luxurious carpet that lined the hall and pretended to be lost in confusion, to give herself time to think.

"I cleaned Master Davis's office this morning," Mary answered. "But I forgot to shine his brass lamp."

O'Melia's eyes narrowed. "Why are you doing it now?" she demanded.

Mary let her own eyes get wide. "Because I just remembered," she said, as if this was the most obvious thing in the world.

O'Melia pursed her lips.

"Turn out your pockets,"

she said.

"My pockets?" Mary repeated. With relief, she realized that O'Melia didn't have any idea what Mary had really been doing in the president's office. O'Melia just thought Mary was a common thief.

Still, deep inside, Mary's pride rankled. O'Melia was a maid just like she was. It wasn't O'Melia's place to question her.

So Mary took her own sweet time obeying O'Melia's order.

Impatient, O'Melia decided to check for herself. She swatted Mary's hands out of the way and pulled out the pockets on either side of Mary's skirt.

To Mary's relief, there was in fact a rag in one of them. That helped prove her story about buffing the brass lamp.

But no matter how hard O'Melia searched, rustling Mary's skirts and yanking her this way and that, she couldn't find anything else.

"You'd best not forget again," O'Melia finally said, her expression still ominous. "Mr. Davis is a very particular man."

"Yes, ma'am," Mary said, staring down at the carpet. "Thank you, ma'am."

Since O'Melia was a fellow servant, Mary didn't need to use this term of respect. But O'Melia ate it up. She lifted her chin and thrust her chest out, and tromped off down the hall as if she'd just won a battle.

As O'Melia turned her back on Mary, Mary finally allowed herself a smile.

O'Melia had no way of knowing that Mary had, in fact, carried something out of the room.

Mary had carried out every dispatch, every report, every letter, and every map that had been on President Davis's desk.

O'Melia didn't know, because she couldn't see them.

All those facts and figures and maps were stored safely in Mary's mind . . .

in her
PHOTOGRAPHIC
memory.

———◦⬦◦———

It was Bet Van Lew who had first come to Mary with the idea that Mary could take the job working at the Confederate White House.

Mary had been born into slavery, in Bet's family. But when Mary was a small girl, Bet, who was a Quaker, had set Mary and all the people who had been slaves of the Van Lew family free.

And Bet had taken a special interest in Mary. She'd made sure that Mary learned how to read, and sent Mary to Philadelphia to school. After that, Mary had worked for a few years as a teacher in Liberia, where other people who had been freed from slavery in America were working to start a new country.

Mary had only come back to Richmond to marry her sweetheart, Wilson Bowser, a servant of the Van Lew family.

But on the day after Mary and Wilson were married, Virginia seceded from the United States. The Southern states, which wanted to preserve slavery as a way of life, broke away from the Union. They declared themselves a whole new country: The Confederate States of America, also known as the Confederacy.

Richmond, where Mary and Wilson lived, was declared the capital of the Confederacy. Jefferson Davis, the president of the Confederacy, moved into a big house in Bet's neighborhood. Quickly, it became known as the Confederate White House.

Just as quickly, Bet Van Lew began to build

a **network** of
S P I E S

in Richmond. She collected every scrap of information she could find that might help the Union generals defeat the Confederacy.

And when she heard that Jefferson Davis's wife, Varina, was looking for a new maid, Bet knew that it was an incredible opportunity. If the right person took the job, she could learn more about the inner workings of the Confederacy than all of Bet's other spies combined.

"I know it's a lot to ask," Bet said when she first brought the idea to Mary.

Mary shook her head. Some part of her was just as thrilled as Bet was with the plan. How many times had she wished there was something she could do to bring an end to slavery?

"But Wilson and I haven't even been married a year," Mary told Bet.

Bet nodded. In her midforties, she was thought of as an old maid by many people in town. But Mary, who was almost twenty years younger than Bet, had always seen a kind of beauty in Bet's strong features and thick dark hair, and she still saw it there now.

"I can't even imagine how hard it would be to leave

him," Bet said. "And I can't even tell you when you could come back home. Nobody knows how long this war will last.

"But I can tell you," Bet added, "that you'll be in a position to change the whole course of this war."

It takes a special kind of smart to play stupid.

If these people weren't so eager to believe that I can't think just as well as them, they wouldn't be so easy to fool.

I miss Wilson. I thought at first that I might die from missing him.

But now that it's been a few months, I realize I miss something else even more.

It was hard to leave Wilson. But it's harder to give up being free.

I haven't had a word from Bet since I took this position.

That was the plan all along. We thought it would be too dangerous for me to start passing her information as soon as I arrived. Too easy for the Confederates to put two and two together, and see that all the evidence for a leak pointed to me.

So I knew it could be months before she reached out.

But now it's been months.

And I can't help wondering: Is this all part of the plan?

Or has something gone terribly wrong?

"**W**here's that new girl?" O'Melia bellowed, bursting into the kitchen.

Mary, who had been doing the dishes from Mrs. Davis's breakfast tray, looked up, trying to hide the flash of annoyance in her eyes.

She'd been there for months, but O'Melia still called her "the new girl." Mary was hardly new anymore. And she was a grown woman, not a girl.

But Mary's annoyance changed to confusion when she saw the vase of rhododendrons she had picked from the garden that morning, bobbing in O'Melia's arms.

The flowers were beautiful, and still fresh. So Mary couldn't figure out why O'Melia would bring them back down to the kitchen already. Or why

O'Melia

grinned like a cat

when she caught sight of Mary.

O'Melia paraded the flowers through the kitchen, then dropped them with a flourish on the counter beside Mary.

"What do you know about the language of flowers?" O'Melia demanded.

Mary had read articles about the language of flowers in women's magazines. It was such a fad these days that it was hard to avoid. But to admit that was to admit she knew how to read.

"Nothing," Mary said.

She'd figured that pretending she was ignorant would please O'Melia, and it did. O'Melia's grin widened. She placed one thick red hand on the counter, striking the pose of a professor before a class.

"It has to do with what the different flowers mean," O'Melia said, as if Mary was a very dull child, and she was a very patient teacher.

"A red rose for love. A daisy for innocence. Like a code."

Mary had to suppress a smile. She'd spent her nights for the past several weeks trying to work out the code the Confederate army used to encrypt their missives.

Not that President Davis decoded them himself. Everything he read was already translated back into the King's English for him. So Mary could read most of it at a glance.

But she was still curious about the few scraps of code she did find, groups of letters that clearly formed words and sentences, but read like utter nonsense.

In comparison, the language of flowers seemed like a children's game.

But O'Melia obviously thought it was dead serious.

And she also seemed to think she had something on Mary.

Something that had to do with the language of flowers.

So Mary played along.

"I didn't know," Mary said. "Thank you for telling me."

"It is not for your education," O'Melia snapped. "Mrs. Davis puts a big store in the language of flowers. Her favorite is the bird-of-paradise. It stands for freedom."

I doubt that means the same thing to her as it does to me, thought Mary.

"But these," O'Melia went on, giving the rhododendrons

a shake. "Would you like to guess why she sent them back the minute she saw them this morning?"

"I don't know," Mary said, her skin pricking with fear. This was the first time she'd ever done anything to displease Mrs. Davis.

"They stand for danger," O'Melia said.

Mary's heart Sank.

"I know you ain't exactly the sharpest tack in the box," O'Melia said. "But even you must have heard how close the Union army is to Richmond. Haven't you?"

Mary nodded. In fact, she probably knew as much about it as some Confederate generals because she had read all the plans of the Confederate army that had crossed President Davis's desk in the past few weeks.

And she knew something else that O'Melia probably didn't know. The Union army had just captured New Orleans, the first step in a plan to split the Confederacy, right down the Mississippi River.

"Mrs. Davis has been real nervous since the new baby was born," O'Melia told Mary. "And Mr. Davis has been nervous for this whole war."

Mary knew this was true as well. More than once, as she'd snuck past the president's bedroom long past midnight, she'd heard Mrs. Davis reading aloud to him because he couldn't sleep.

"Now the Union army is knocking on the door," O'Melia went on. "A sign of danger is the last thing she wants to see this morning."

"I'm sorry," Mary said, despite how much it galled her

to have to apologize to O'Melia. "I didn't know."

"I told her you was slow," O'Melia said. Her eyes glowed with pleasure as she delivered this insult. "And she knows you're new. That's the only reason she didn't put you right out on the street this morning."

O'Melia shook her head as Mary opened her mouth.

"Don't thank me," she said. "You've still got your job, for now. But she'll have her eye on you. We both will."

———◦◦◇◇◇◦◦———

O'Melia was as good as her word.

Mary knew that O'Melia had been watching her ever since she arrived.

But now O'Melia actually seemed to *be* everywhere Mary was.

Time and again, Mary would step out of a room, or come around a corner, to find O'Melia waiting, her sharp eyes narrow.

Other times, O'Melia seemed to appear out of nowhere. Mary would be working quietly in a room, sure she had the place to herself, and suddenly O'Melia would be there, almost as if she'd managed to

pass   right   up

through the floorboards,

like a GHOST.

Each time she visited President Davis's personal office, Mary learned to double back two or three times, so that she'd run into O'Melia if O'Melia was following her.

To be safe, Mary often scanned the Confederate plans as she was actually buffing the brass or polishing the rich wood of the desk.

And Mary's precautions seemed to pay off. Despite all the times O'Melia surprised Mary at her other work, she never caught her looking at anything on the president's desk.

But O'Melia did catch Mary doing something almost as bad.

Mary couldn't help herself.

The work as a maid was deadly boring, carrying the same trays and cleaning the same rooms every day.

And Mary loved to read.

She'd loved it ever since she first learned as a child.

And other than the plans of the Confederate leadership, she hadn't been able to read anything since she arrived at the Davis home.

So when she saw that Mrs. Davis had left a copy of a new book by one of Mary's favorite authors on the table by Mrs. Davis's bed, Mary couldn't resist.

She sank down on a chair and lost herself in the first few pages.

Until she heard an all-too-familiar voice.

"That a good book?" O'Melia asked.

Her question dragged Mary back from the thrilling

story to the harsh reality in an instant.

In another instant,

Mary REALIZED

how much

DANGER

she was in.

Even though O'Melia hadn't caught her rifling through the president's papers, O'Melia had caught Mary committing another crime.

In the state of Virginia, it was illegal to teach people in slavery to read or write.

And now that the Union and the Confederacy were at war, Mary could pay for that crime with her life. And so could Bet, if the connection between the two of them was found out.

Mary jumped to her feet, making a big show of distress, which wasn't hard. Her heart really was pounding. And her quick mind raced.

"Oh, no, ma'am," she said. "I can't read. I just like to look at the pictures."

Thankfully, the book had been open to a beautiful illustration of a young couple boating on a small lake under the shade of tall trees.

Mary turned the book to O'Melia to show her. "I know I shouldn't look at Mrs. Davis's book," she said. "But it was just so pretty. See?"

O'Melia's sharp eyes scanned Mary's face.

"I can't tell if you're as dumb as you look," she said. "Or a sight too smart for your own good."

———◦∞◇∞◦———

Mary couldn't sleep that night for worry.

But the next morning, she was awakened by a commotion in the yard.

When she dressed and went out, she found the president and Mrs. Davis, along with most of the other slaves and servants. They were all gathered around a carriage that was piled high with boxes for a long journey.

Mrs. Davis's eyes were red with tears.

"I don't want to go," she told her husband. "What will people think if the president of the Confederacy can't even keep his own family safe in Richmond?"

Mary watched her closely. Mrs. Davis wasn't always easy to work for, but Mary had sized her up as a smart woman with her own independent thoughts. And it was no secret among the servants that Mrs. Davis had doubts that the Confederacy could win the war.

In fact, Mary had discovered from the president's letters, the leaders of the Confederacy sometimes went out of their way to remind the president that the less his wife knew about their plans, the better.

So Mary knew that Mrs. Davis probably had no idea why the president was making her leave town.

But Mary did.

From reading Davis's papers, she knew that a huge storm was brewing over Richmond, the Confederate capital. All spring, General McClellan, the leader of the Union

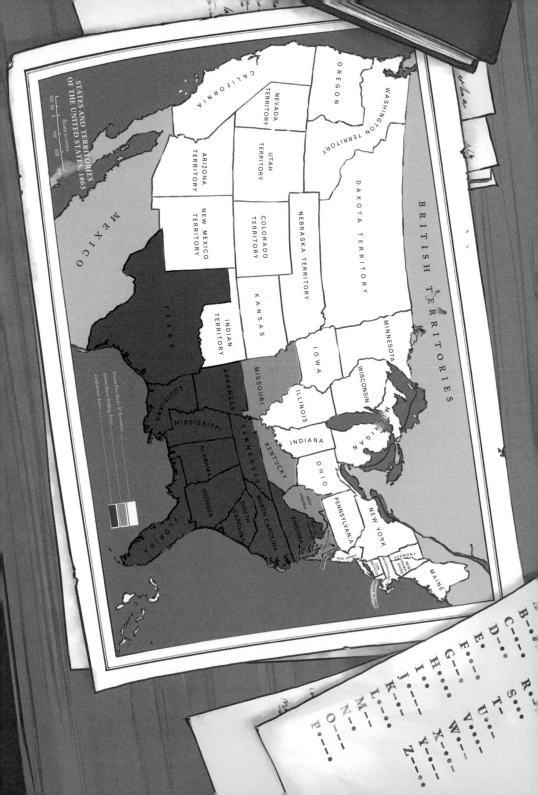

army, had been fighting his way toward Richmond. And for weeks now, the Union army had been on Richmond's doorstep, just waiting for the spring rains to end so that they wouldn't be bogged down in mud on their final march to capture the city.

General Johnston, the leader of the Confederate forces, didn't seem to be able to do anything to stop General McClellan's advance on Richmond. Again and again, Johnston had fallen back when McClellan attacked. The leaders of the Confederacy weren't happy about this. And Mary had read a lot of talk about replacing General Johnston with Robert E. Lee, who had been a hero in the United States army before he joined the Confederacy.

But whoever wound up in charge, Richmond faced a huge battle over its fate.

Still, Mrs. Davis was no coward. And she didn't want to leave her husband.

"I don't want to go," Mrs. Davis insisted, tears of frustration running down her face. "And neither do the children. We're not afraid."

"It's settled," Davis told her. "You'll leave today. As I already told you."

Then, at the back of the coach, Mary caught sight of another figure.

The face was familiar enough, but it took Mary a moment to recognize her, because she was dressed in traveling clothes, not the maid's uniform she always wore in the house.

It was O'Melia.

Wherever Mrs. Davis was going, apparently O'Melia was going, too.

Almost as if she could feel Mary's gaze on her, O'Melia turned around.

Her eyes locked with Mary's.

Mary could see all the suspicion in O'Melia's expression, and all the threat.

And to keep playing the role of the simpleminded servant, Mary ducked her head as if she couldn't see what O'Melia meant.

But inside, Mary's heart soared.

Because as soon as the carriage set out, O'Melia would be far away.

Too far away to follow Mary's every move.

At least for now.

———◦◦◇◦◦———

With Mrs. Davis and the children and most of the servants gone, the house was strangely quiet.

Sometimes, as Mary padded alone through the halls, she had the eerie sense that she and the other slaves and servants might have turned into ghosts, haunting a house where no one lived anymore.

But with O'Melia gone, Mary had the run of the place. Which meant that she could read virtually everything that now came across President Davis's home desk.

And events quickly proved that Davis had been wise to send his family south.

By the end of May 1862, the Union's General McClellan and his army had reached the outskirts of Richmond. Confederate General Johnston attacked McClellan's Union forces on the last day of May.

The two armies fought a huge battle with terrible casualties on both sides. And General Johnston himself was wounded.

That was all the excuse Confederate leaders needed to replace General Johnston with General Lee.

For several weeks that June, McClellan nursed his army's wounds.

And General Lee built up Richmond's defenses and his own Army of Northern Virginia.

Then Lee exploded into action. He drove the Union army away from Richmond in seven bloody days of battle.

The Confederate leadership was jubilant. General Lee was a hero to the South.

But Mary's heart sank as she read the news.

As the Union army had inched closer to Richmond that spring, she had hoped that the war might be over soon.

She could go back to her husband, Wilson.

She could live as a free person.

And so could the four million other people who now lived in slavery.

But Mary was smart enough to understand what the reports of Lee's victory meant.

The W A R wasn't over yet.

And it might not be, for a good long time.

———◦⟨◇⟩◦———

Mrs. Davis was gone.

But all her winter dresses, and half her summer

dresses, were still in Richmond.

So it was decided that now was the time to have all of them repaired and refashioned.

Since the war had begun, it was harder and harder to get new fabrics and sewing notions. Mrs. Davis still dressed beautifully, even as the people of Richmond began to scrimp and save. But even Mrs. Davis needed to have her dresses repaired now: the hems redone, the collars and cuffs turned over so that the worn parts didn't show.

So every few days, Mary took an armful of gowns to a seamstress across town.

These walks were a little taste of freedom, away from the house, where she was able to choose her own path for a change.

And the shop reminded Mary of other, better days, when she had been the one who ordered dresses, and not a servant. She always felt a bit more at ease when she stepped inside.

Which might explain why it was so easy for

someone to

S N E A K   U P

on her from behind one morning.

———◦⬦◦———

The touch on her shoulder was light, even gentle.

But Mary jerked in surprise and dropped the dresses she'd brought on the dressmaker's counter.

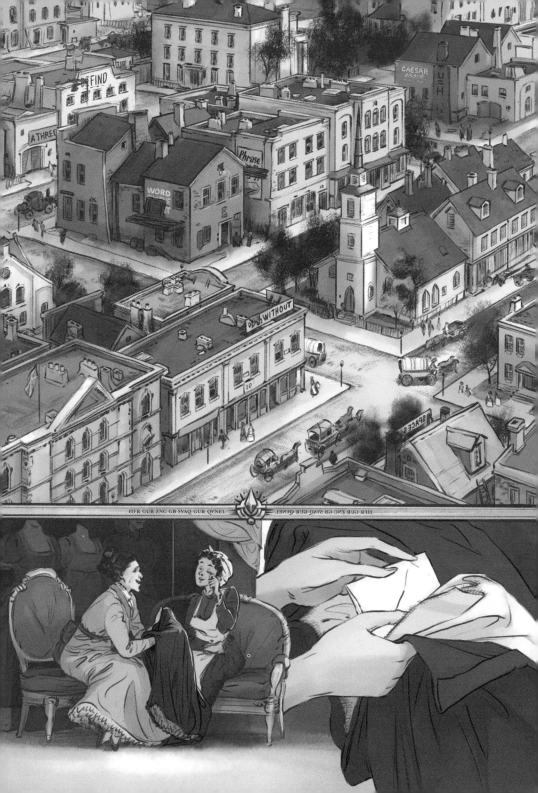

Don't forget
your act,
Mary told herself as she
spun around.

But as soon as she saw the woman behind her, Mary ignored her own advice.

She grinned with delight, dropping the act of dim-witted servant that she'd been playing for the better part of a year. "Bet," she said.

It was the first time the two of them had seen each other since the previous Christmas, when Mary first took the job in the Confederate White House—and became a spy.

Mary took a step toward Bet, following an instinct to embrace her.

Then she caught herself and looked around the shop.

It was empty except for the two of them.

Bet nodded toward the back.

"I've arranged a private fitting for us," she said evenly.

Mary followed Bet around the dressmaker's counter, through the pair of velvet curtains that hid the back rooms of the shop.

Surrounded by dresses, the two of them sank down on a couch.

They stared at each other for a long moment. Mary's heart and mind were so full that she couldn't think of anything to say.

"How are you doing?" Bet asked.

Nobody had spoken to Mary with such kindness in months. It brought tears to Mary's eyes. But she quickly blinked them back.

"I'm collecting all kinds of information," she told Bet. "Everything I can find on the president's desk."

"I know it's been a long time since we spoke," Bet said. "And I'm afraid we don't have a long time now. But I've got a plan for you to get the information you've gathered to me. A seamstress here has agreed to act as our go-between."

Bet pulled back the lining of a nearby dress.

"When you have messages," she told Mary, "just slip them inside the lining. The seamstress will check each dress you deliver for information."

Mary nodded.

"And there's another way," Bet added. "I've been building a network of informants in Richmond. Thomas McNiven is one of them."

"The redheaded baker," Mary said. She knew him: a brash Scotsman who made regular deliveries of shortbread, cookies, and scones to the Davis household.

Bet nodded. "He'll also carry any message you have to me."

Quickly Mary shared all the information she had collected over the past months with Bet. She told her about the fights she'd read about between Confederate leaders. She told her the secret military plans she'd read. And she told Bet about Davis himself: his worry, depression, and sleeplessness.

Then Mary couldn't stand it any longer. "How is Wilson?" she finally asked.

Bet's expression, which had been strictly business a moment ago, softened.

"HE'S SAFE,"
Bet said, squeezing Mary's hand.

"He's living at our family farm outside town. He's been working for the Union, like you. In fact, he's been ferrying information to the Union boats on the Appomattox by night. He'll take this information you've just given me. There aren't too many men who could navigate those woods and that river in the dark."

To her surprise, Mary felt tears in her eyes. "No," she agreed, her heart tugging as she thought about Wilson's bravery—and the danger he was in. "There aren't."

"There's just one other thing," Bet said.

With effort, Mary brought herself back to the present. "What's that?" she asked.

"I need you to look for something for me," Bet said. "A cipher."

"All the messages that come across President Davis's desk are already decoded for him," Mary told her. "He can't read the codes himself."

Bet sighed. "Too many of the messages that fall into my hands are still in code," she said. "Until I find the cipher and the key, I can't read them. I have no idea how much they might help the Union if we could."

Mary shook her head. "I don't think I've ever seen anything like that," she said.

"Look for me," Bet said. "And send anything that might have something to do with a code. It might seem like non-

sense. In fact, it probably will."

Mary nodded.

Outside, in the main room of the store, the shop bell rang.

Mary rose. "We can't be seen together," she said.

Bet stood as well, while Mary's mind raced to make sure they'd talked about everything. She knew it could be days, or weeks, before she could get another message to Bet.

Which made her realize something.

"Wait," she said. "We need a signal."

"What do you mean?" Bet asked.

"In case I have urgent information," Mary said. "Something the Union should know as soon as possible."

Bet nodded. "That would be wise," she agreed.

"Can you pass by the Davis house every day?" Mary asked.

Bet lived in the same neighborhood, Mary calculated. So that shouldn't be too dangerous for Bet—or for Mary.

"I can arrange that," Bet said.

"Then watch for a red shirt hanging in the front window," Mary said. "If you see one, it means I'll have a message for you right away. Here, at the dress shop."

"I'll be watching," Bet promised.

Until now, it hasn't quite seemed real. I've spent so much time working in this house that sometimes it seems like the only life I've ever known.

But now that I've seen Bet, I know that everything I can find here will wind up in the right hands.

That it will get to the people who can do something about it.

That everything I've done, and everything I've given up, will mean something.

I'm so glad to know that Wilson's safe. And to know where he is.

But in some ways it's harder to know that than to know nothing at all.

He's so close. It wouldn't even take me the afternoon to reach him.

And my heart keeps asking, if he's so close, why can't we be together?

But we both know why. Because there are some things that are more important than just him and me.

It warms my heart to know that he's the one who will take the information I've gathered to the Union boats.

Even if we can't see each other, it's almost as if we're still together.

Both working for freedom.

So every time I sew a new report into one of Mrs. Davis's dresses, I'm not just sending a message to Bet.

I know Wilson will help deliver it, too.

And I like to think everything I send to Bet and everything he ferries to the Union boats are a strange kind of love letter, from me to him.

Mrs. Davis and the children returned to Richmond that fall, just as news of President Lincoln's Emancipation Proclamation spread through the city.

Lincoln's order, whispered from person to person by the house staff, proclaimed that if the Confederacy did not rejoin the Union by January, all people held as slaves in the rebel states would be free in the Union's eyes.

The rumor caused an uproar in the house. For weeks it was all anyone talked about.

But as Mary searched through the papers on President Davis's desk, she got another perspective. She saw what the Confederate leaders thought of Lincoln's proclamation.

And it hadn't made them more eager for peace. If anything, they seemed even more determined now to fight to the death.

Some of the messages Mary read on Davis's desk were full of indignation: How dare the Union tell us what to do?

But other messages spoke of the growing fear of slave owners. If the four million people who currently lived in slavery in the South were suddenly set free, what would happen?

How would the fields get worked? What would happen to all the millions and millions of dollars slave owners had spent buying people, if those people were set free? And most important, what would all those people do?

Mary even read a copy of Lincoln's proclamation that had been sent to Davis. Her heart burned as she read the words of freedom.

But her head reminded her that Lincoln's words hadn't actually set one person in the Davis household free. All the slaves Davis owned were still working for the family, just as they always had.

If Mr. Lincoln wants to set us free, Mary thought, *he has to do more than talk. We have to win this war.*

———◦◦◇◦◦———

Mary braced herself when the family first returned. For several days, she lived on edge, expecting to find O'Melia lurking again around every corner.

I'm so worried about O'Melia that I'm doing her work for her, Mary thought. *She doesn't even have to follow me around to get me tied up in knots.*

Maybe it was because of all the parties.

All fall and winter, Richmond was a whirl of dinners and balls, many of them at the Davis mansion. The whole staff was busy cooking, serving, mending, pressing, and cleaning up after the constant stream of well-dressed men and women.

As young officers tried to impress young ladies with their plans, or generals murmured strategy to each other over port, Mary set down trays of food, carried off plates—and listened.

Always listening.

Everything she heard went in her reports to Bet. Some she sewed into the hems and linings of Mrs. Davis's dresses. Others she slipped to Thomas McNiven, the baker, who she now went out to greet every time his cart rolled up to the Davis home.

But after months of searching, she still hadn't found anything that might help Bet crack the Confederate code.

Then one night as she and O'Melia collected coats from the arriving guests, Mary took one from a Confederate officer that was strangely heavy. A quick glance inside revealed a thick cache of documents poking out of an inner pocket.

Mary's heart skipped a beat.

But how could she get a look at them?

She could hardly read through them with O'Melia at her side.

And she knew that, after she and O'Melia left the room, she wouldn't be able to get back alone. She had been chosen to serve dinner, and dessert, and drinks to the gentlemen when the meal was over.

So when O'Melia's back was turned, Mary turned the handsome military jacket upside down and dumped all the papers out.

They scattered everywhere.

"Oh no!" Mary said, kneeling quickly to get a look at as many of them as she could.

"You stupid girl," O'Melia said, coming over to investigate. "You'd better get those picked up before the next guests arrive."

Mary made a show of scrabbling around to pick up every page. And of being very clumsy while she did it, to give herself as much time as possible with each one.

Some of them seemed familiar, copies of documents she had read on the president's desk.

But several of them were clearly in cipher. She had seen almost none of this before, because all communications came to Davis already translated. But as Mary stared down at the ciphered sentences, she felt some of the same anxious curiosity that had driven Bet to ask for Mary's help breaking the code.

"What in the world is that?" O'Melia asked, her brow furrowing.

Mary looked up at her, wide-eyed. "What?" she asked, as if she couldn't tell the difference between plain English and the ciphered letters herself.

O'Melia shook her head in disgust.

Then she poked her toe at a stray paper under a divan. "You missed one," O'Melia said.

It took everything Mary had not to cry out with excitement when she picked up the last paper. Instead of a collection of sentences, this was a

g r i d of l e t t e r s .

And from the crumpled page and the pen dots around each line, Mary was sure that it had been well used—

for

breaking
C O D E .

———◦◦◦◦◦———

Very early the next morning Mary slipped into the pantry, where she knew no one would see her writing, and copied the entire grid of letters down from memory.

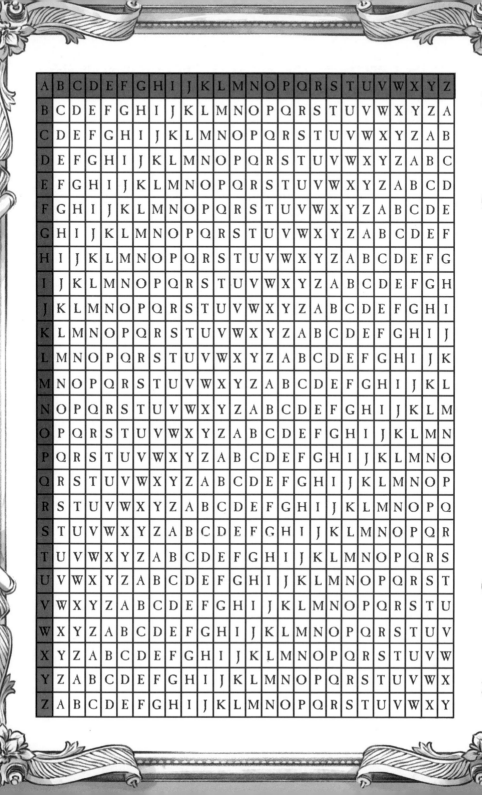

When Thomas McNiven arrived with his morning delivery, she was at the back gate, waiting.

And as he passed her a wrapped box full of bread and scones, she passed him the paper, folded so small that it fit into the palm of his hand.

The next morning, McNiven was back, his grin big.

"I've got a little something for you," he said, handing her a round butter cookie. "We had a few left over this morning."

Mary started to take a bite, but something in McNiven's expression stopped her.

"It's got a little something special in it," he said with a wink. "My own recipe."

Mary dropped the cookie into her pocket.

As she walked away with McNiven's box of baked goods, she crumbled the hidden cookie to pieces. As the butter and flour disintegrated in her pocket, she felt a piece of paper.

She unfolded it in the pantry, her chest tight with excitement. Had she finally found the missing piece Bet needed?

I'm glad for your message, Bet had scrawled. *It appears to be a* **Vigenère cipher**. *But it works with a* **key word or phrase**. *Until we have that, we can't crack the code. Can you find us anything else?*

By early spring, the Union blockade, which prevented any food or goods from coming in or out of Richmond, began to pinch the city.

Mrs. Davis had nice things long after they disappeared from the streets of Richmond: new dresses, paper, books, coffee. Mary even served the Davis family a pineapple one night, smuggled in for the Confederate president all the way from Bermuda.

But now it had gotten so bad that Mrs. Davis had begun to economize, ordering a new pair of gloves made from one of her husband's old suits.

Outside, the city was STARVING.

At the beginning of April, there was a huge commotion at the front door.

Mary, O'Melia, and two other servants all arrived at the same time.

Whoever was outside didn't just knock a few times, then stop. They pounded and pounded on the door until O'Melia swung it open.

By this time, President Davis himself had come halfway down the stairs from his office. He looked in shock at the young man who stood in the doorway, his hair disheveled, panting.

"President Davis," he said. "You've got to come quick. The people are rioting in the streets."

"What for?" Davis asked, hurrying down the rest of the steps.

"Bread," the man said.

Davis didn't return for hours.

When he did, he went straight up to see his wife.

Mary, who was cleaning a nearby room, drifted down the hall to eavesdrop.

"I spoke with them," Davis said. "They listened."

But that wasn't the story Mary heard later that day, from a servant who had been out on the street during the disturbance.

"Mr. Davis made a real nice speech," he said. "But it was an ugly crowd. So he told his own men to fire on them if they wouldn't go home."

"Serves them right," O'Melia said. "Rabble-rousing in the streets."

The other servant kept silent until O'Melia left the room.

But when she did, he added, "It's a funny way to win a war. Firing on your own people."

Donelson.

Nashville.

Memphis.

As each of the Southern cities

had fallen to Union forces during the previous year, President Davis had become more and more despondent. More nights than not now, Mrs. Davis had to read to him for hours before he could fall asleep.

Sick and distracted, he went into the capitol less and less, and spent more and more time at his home desk.

Which meant that even more papers now piled up in his office for Mary to read and report to Bet.

In May, Mary caught sight of the president sitting at his desk, head in his hands. When she passed by a few minutes later, he was still in the same position, as if he'd been frozen there.

As soon as she could get free of her other duties, she hurried back.

Davis had finally left his desk. It was obvious from the messages scattered across it that the Confederacy had suffered some terrible blow.

As Mary read them, she drew in her breath.

The messages reported the death of Stonewall Jackson, one of the Confederacy's most important generals.

He had been shot accidentally by his own soldiers.

Mary had read enough of the past years' reports to know how important Jackson had been to the Confederate army. Over and over again, it had been Jackson's stubborn fighting spirit that had helped General Lee win his victories.

But instead of bowing her head in distress, like President Davis, she felt hope stir in her heart.

Without General Jackson, could General Lee fight on for long?

———◦◇◇◦———

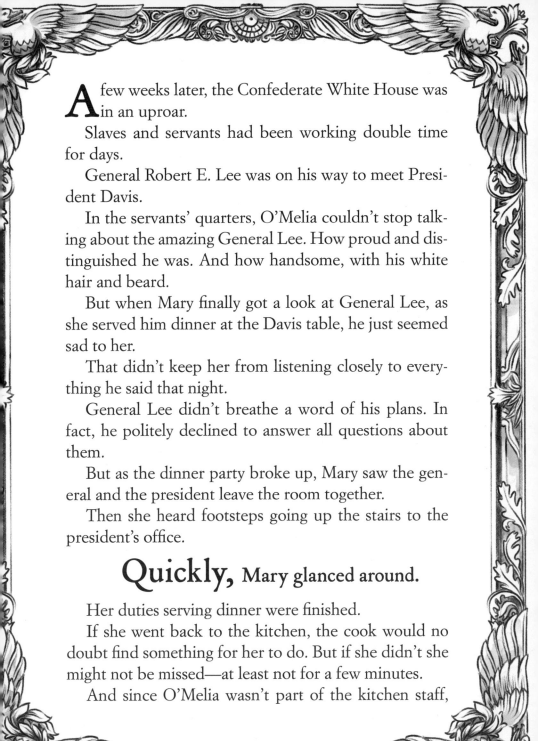

A few weeks later, the Confederate White House was in an uproar.

Slaves and servants had been working double time for days.

General Robert E. Lee was on his way to meet President Davis.

In the servants' quarters, O'Melia couldn't stop talking about the amazing General Lee. How proud and distinguished he was. And how handsome, with his white hair and beard.

But when Mary finally got a look at General Lee, as she served him dinner at the Davis table, he just seemed sad to her.

That didn't keep her from listening closely to everything he said that night.

General Lee didn't breathe a word of his plans. In fact, he politely declined to answer all questions about them.

But as the dinner party broke up, Mary saw the general and the president leave the room together.

Then she heard footsteps going up the stairs to the president's office.

Quickly, Mary glanced around.

Her duties serving dinner were finished.

If she went back to the kitchen, the cook would no doubt find something for her to do. But if she didn't she might not be missed—at least not for a few minutes.

And since O'Melia wasn't part of the kitchen staff,

she wasn't there at dinner to watch Mary's every move.

When Mary slipped upstairs to the president's office, the two men's voices were already raised so loud that she could hear them easily through the closed door.

They were arguing over someplace in Pennsylvania she'd never heard of before.

"We've let them fight too many battles on our soil," Lee was saying. "We need to take the war to them. Our farms need time to recover if we don't want our land ruined. And

our army needs supplies. Supplies we can find if we move north."

"But who will defend Richmond if the army goes north?" Davis objected.

Mary heard a sound that might have been a fist thumping on a desk. But she couldn't be sure whose it was.

"My men are tired of fighting to defend," Lee insisted. "It's time to fight to win."

"The risk is so great," Davis said.

"But so is the prize," Lee said. "With a foothold in Pennsylvania, we're only days away from Philadelphia and Baltimore."

Mary drew in her breath.

"And Washington," Lee added.

Mary **heard**
S O M E T H I N G
stir behind her.

Someone was moving around in one of the nearby rooms.

But that didn't make sense, Mary calculated.

She was absolutely certain that all the children had been corralled in the nursery for the night. And all the ladies were still downstairs, at dinner.

Then she realized: O'Melia wasn't serving dinner.

But that didn't mean she had retired to the servants' quarters.

In fact, there was every reason to believe that it was O'Melia rummaging around, cleaning up after the mess the ladies had made as they got ready.

And there was no excuse that would satisfy O'Melia if she discovered Mary eavesdropping on the president's conversation with the general.

In a flash, Mary slipped back down the stairs, and back into the dining room.

Her return, just like her departure, didn't seem to attract any attention.

They never noticed I was gone, she thought to herself. *Because they never really knew I was here.*

For the rest of the night, she continued to play her part of the dim-witted, dutiful servant.

Except for the moment she slipped away to hang

a RED SHIRT in the window.

———⬦⬦⬦———

Mary passed on what she'd heard to Bet the next day in a hurried meeting at the dress shop.

And then she waited.

Every day, she slipped into Davis's office to read the reports he'd left on his desk. Sometimes she even found his papers lying around the house. She'd heard Davis's colleagues beseech him about this once, asking him to take more care with the new nation's secrets.

But Davis apparently couldn't believe that anyone who worked in his home might ever turn against him.

So Mary was often able to read sensitive documents without even sneaking into his office, just in the course of her daily chores around the house.

As long as no one caught her reading, of course.

And that was **easier said than done.**

O'Melia seemed to want Mary to think that she had stopped watching her at all.

But Mary knew better. Every time she looked at O'Melia, O'Melia was looking at her. And no matter where Mary went in the house, O'Melia was always a little too close.

She didn't pop out from around corners anymore. But she was always disappearing down the hall just as Mary came by. And she moved so quietly that Mary was constantly looking over her shoulder, even when O'Melia was nowhere to be found.

But one day, as Mary had just picked up a handful of papers President Davis had left in the sitting room, she felt a pricking at the back of her neck.

When she turned around, there was O'Melia.

Because O'Melia knew that Mary had only just picked up the papers, Mary made a big show of wiping off the table they had been sitting on.

She shook her head theatrically. "Mr. Davis is always leaving his papers around," she said. "I swear, it's twice as much work to get the dusting done with his things everywhere you look."

But from the expression on O'Melia's face, Mary could see that she hadn't bought a word of it.

"You sure have a lot of interest in books and papers," O'Melia said. "For a girl who doesn't know how to read."

Through the reports to the president, Mary watched Lee's plan play out, day by day.

The gathering of the troops.

The drive up through Confederate territory, to the north.

Then, on July 1, battle reports began to pour in from Gettysburg.

The news was sickening for Mary to read.

On the first day of fighting, the Union line collapsed.

Mary snuck back to her room that night with her head full of thoughts and prayers and fears.

She wondered how long the war would last if the Union lost this battle to Lee.

And she tried not to even think about what might happen to her, and all of her people, if the Confederacy won the war.

But by the second day, reinforcements arrived from the North.

This time, the Union line fought off everything that Lee threw at them.

And on the third day, the Union line still held against more than ten thousand infantry that Lee sent in a charge against the center of the Union forces.

By that night, July 3, Lee had lost four of every ten men in his army.

There was nothing for him to do but retreat in defeat.

The next day, on the Fourth of July, Davis received news of another blow to the Confederacy.

After a six-week siege, the Confederate stronghold of Vicksburg, in Mississippi, had finally surrendered to the Union general Ulysses S. Grant.

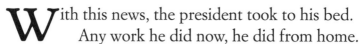

With this news, the president took to his bed. Any work he did now, he did from home.

So now every paper that passed through his hands also passed through Mary's.

Then from Mary's hands straight to the Union.

And the Confederacy was starting to realize it.

Letters to Davis now talked openly about suspicions that there was a spy in the upper reaches of the Confederacy.

Each time the spy was mentioned, Mary felt a pang of fear that she might be discovered.

But she also felt a thrill of accomplishment.

And then, one day, she found a letter that President Davis had started, but left half-finished on his desk.

"No printed paper can be kept secret," he complained.

Mary's eyes glowed with satisfaction.

That's because of me, she thought. *And he doesn't know it.*

But in the months following the Battle of Gettysburg, Thomas McNiven slipped Mary another message from Bet.

BEWARE, it read.

Suspicion has fallen on me. Take care it does not fall on you.

Before, Mary wrote reports for Bet at night, then sewed them into one of Mrs. Davis's dresses in the morning.

Now Mary made sure that each report was sewn up and delivered to the dressmaker's shop as soon as she wrote it. She was taking no chances that anyone else might find something she'd written.

She had been in the habit of pressing messages into Thomas McNiven's hand when she went out to meet his bakery wagon.

Now she tucked the messages carefully between the slats of his cart as she lifted the boxes of pastries out. She didn't want anybody to catch sight of something passing between them.

Mary was most careful with the best evidence against her: the diary and pen that proved she knew how to read and write. Ever since she had arrived, she had kept them hidden under the pallet she slept on.

Now she started to hide them outside her room, tucked in out-of-the-way corners somewhere else in the house. And she started to move them every few days. She didn't want anybody to find them by a simple search of her things.

As the fall dragged on, Mary was glad she had taken precautions.

Every few days now, she returned to her space and had the uneasy feeling that someone else had already been there.

It wasn't that anything was out of place.

It was that everything was just a bit too neat.

It felt like another maid had pawed through Mary's things but couldn't resist showing off her skills as a maid by tidying up before she left.

And that could only mean one thing: O'Melia.

I used to write these notes before I went to bed.

Now I write them anywhere I can. And anytime, whenever I get a minute to myself, before I find another hiding place for this journal.

Today, I'm writing at President Davis's desk.

He is still sleeping this morning. O'Melia is out with Mrs. Davis and her family, and everyone else is downstairs.

This spring will be my third in this house. I've been here more than two years now.

That seems like a long time when I think about everything I left behind.

But then I think about how much has changed since I came here.

And it doesn't seem like such a long time for the whole world to end. And a new one to begin.

That spring, Union forces camped so close to Richmond that Richmond's starving people could hear the constant thunder of guns.

And because they were so close, it was even easier for Bet to get the information Mary gave her to the Union leadership.

"Anything you tell me is on the desk of a Union general that same day," Bet told Mary in a meeting at the dress shop. Bet smiled wryly. "Sometimes I even send them flowers from my own garden. They're so close that the blooms are still fresh when they arrive."

Mary allowed herself a rare smile in return.

"But I still wish we could crack the Confederate code," Bet said. "Have you had any luck finding the key?"

⸻◇◇◇◇⸻

Mary hadn't.

The thought had never been far from her mind as she sifted through Davis's papers. But she'd never found anything that seemed to relate to the Confederate code.

The letters that crossed Davis's desk now warned the president of starvation and low morale among Confederate troops.

In September, Atlanta fell to the Union.

Davis drew up a plan to raid Union prisons and free the thousands of Confederate soldiers who had been taken captive in Atlanta.

This time, Mary didn't wait for the evening to write the report to Bet.

The instant she discovered Davis's plan, Mary scrawled down the details and passed them to Thomas McNiven on his morning visit.

"The scones smell good this morning," she told him, making sure that he saw the paper she wedged into the slats of his wagon.

"You can always trust me to make a delivery," McNiven said.

———◦◦◇◦◦———

The next morning, Mary could hear Davis's voice, raised in frustration, as she listened outside his office door. "I conceived of this raid yesterday," he complained to one of his staff. "By the afternoon, it was common knowledge in Richmond's streets. Cancel the plans.

We can't win if they know our every move in advance."

Mary slipped away down the hall, her heart pounding.

In all the years she had risked her life as a Union spy, this was the first time she knew for certain that it had made a difference.

———◦◦◇◦◦———

That fall, the Union army marched through Georgia to the sea, from Atlanta to Savannah, leaving a trail of scorched earth behind.

Mary continued to report every message that arrived for Davis.

And every night when she went back to her own things, she could tell that O'Melia had been through them yet again.

For the first time, Mary understood what it might be like for Davis to sit down at his desk every day, not sure where the leak in his leadership was coming from, or how to stop it.

Every time she pulled her diary from a new hiding place, she stopped to wonder: *Is this exactly how I left these pages? Has anyone touched them but me?*

Every time she returned to her room, she tried to read the folds of her blanket, or the dust on the floor, for clues: When had O'Melia been there? What did she see?

It was enough to drive a person crazy.

<hr />

By Christmas, all of Richmond was starving. Not even the first family of the Confederacy had enough to eat.

Every day, Mary still slipped into the president's office, hoping to find some piece of information that would help bring an end to the war—or break the Confederate code.

Then one day, as she quickly sifted the president's papers, she noticed something scrawled in the margin of an especially sensitive report: *Manchester Bluff.*

It caught her attention because she had seen it at least once before, in the margin of another top secret document, months earlier.

She'd thought it had just been a careless note. And she hadn't been able to connect the words to any of the battles she knew about.

But now that it appeared a second time, she looked closer. And this time, she saw something more.

A series of small dots appeared around the letters, very much like someone had been

counting them, over and over.

And very much like the small dots that had appeared on the block for the Vigenère cipher.

———◦◦◇◦◦———

She caught Thomas McNiven that morning just as he was pulling away from the house.

"Well, missy," he said, drawing up his horses. "What can I do for you today?" His face was as amiable as ever, but Mary could see that her unexpected visit made him nervous.

It made her nervous, too.

But if she had found the key to the Confederate cipher, there was no time to waste.

She glanced around the yard, which appeared to be deserted.

"I'll be at the dress shop today," she said quickly. "It's important."

McNiven's gaze shifted. From the way he looked past her, Mary knew someone must have appeared in the yard behind her.

And before Mary turned, she knew it must be O'Melia.

To Mary's relief, O'Melia was too far away to have heard what Mary said.

But not too far away to see Mary and McNiven together.

"You'll tell her," Mary said.

McNiven didn't respond.

Instead, he tipped his hat to O'Melia. But O'Melia's steely expression didn't change.

"Helping with the delivery?" O'Melia asked, as McNiven drove off and Mary walked back to the house.

Distracted, Mary nodded.

O'Melia took a hard look at Mary's empty hands.

"So where is it?" she asked.

"Oh," Mary said. "I already made one trip. I just came back to see if he had anything else. He didn't."

O'Melia's eyes narrowed.

As Mary walked to the house, she could feel them burning into her back.

———◦◦◇◇◦◦———

"**D**oes it work?" Mary asked. "Does it crack the code?"

Bet pulled a sheaf of papers from her pocket.

"We'll see," she said, spreading them out on a low table in the back of the dress shop.

Quickly, Bet explained how the Vigenère code key worked.

If someone wanted to change a word, such as *Lee*, into code, they would go to the first letter of the key word on the horizontal row of the cipher.

If the key phrase was *Manchester Bluff*, as Mary sus-

pected, the first letter would be *M*.

Then the coder would go to the letter *L*, for *Lee*, in the vertical column of the cipher. He would follow that vertical column down the page, until it met the horizontal line that began with *M*, from *Manchester*.

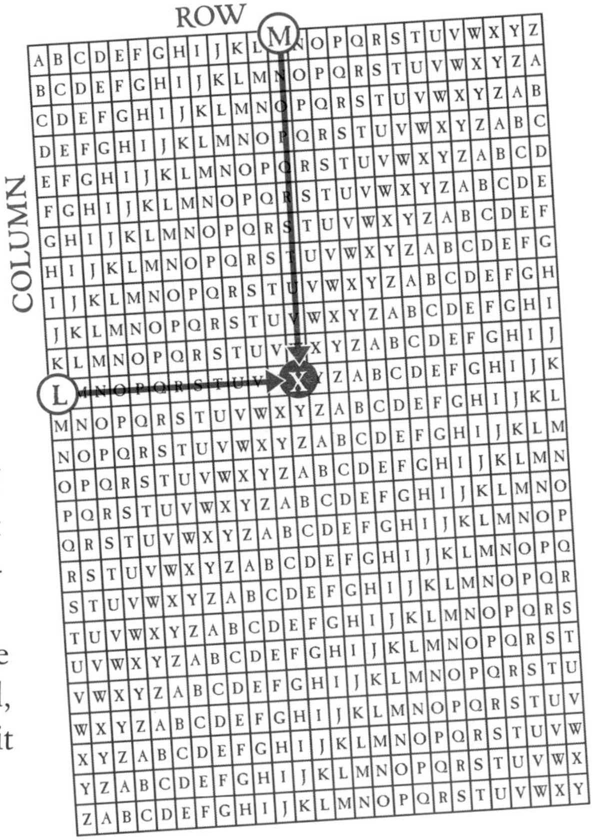

Where those two lines converged in the cipher block lay the letter *X*. That would be the first letter of the encryption.

For encoding longer messages, the coders would use every letter of *Manchester Bluff*. When they came to the end of the phrase, they just started back at the beginning again, with *M*.

"So to break the code," Mary reasoned, "we just have to work it backward."

"Exactly," said Bet.

ROW / COLUMN cipher block

```
ROW
A B C D E F G H I J K L M N O P Q R S T U V W X Y Z
B C D E F G H I J K L M N O P Q R S T U V W X Y Z A
C D E F G H I J K L M N O P Q R S T U V W X Y Z A B
D E F G H I J K L M N O P Q R S T U V W X Y Z A B C
E F G H I J K L M N O P Q R S T U V W X Y Z A B C D
F G H I J K L M N O P Q R S T U V W X Y Z A B C D E
G H I J K L M N O P Q R S T U V W X Y Z A B C D E F
H I J K L M N O P Q R S T U V W X Y Z A B C D E F G
I J K L M N O P Q R S T U V W X Y Z A B C D E F G H
J K L M N O P Q R S T U V W X Y Z A B C D E F G H I
K L M N O P Q R S T U V W X Y Z A B C D E F G H I J
L M N O P Q R S T U V W X Y Z A B C D E F G H I J K
M N O P Q R S T U V W X Y Z A B C D E F G H I J K L
N O P Q R S T U V W X Y Z A B C D E F G H I J K L M
O P Q R S T U V W X Y Z A B C D E F G H I J K L M N
P Q R S T U V W X Y Z A B C D E F G H I J K L M N O
Q R S T U V W X Y Z A B C D E F G H I J K L M N O P
R S T U V W X Y Z A B C D E F G H I J K L M N O P Q
S T U V W X Y Z A B C D E F G H I J K L M N O P Q R
T U V W X Y Z A B C D E F G H I J K L M N O P Q R S
U V W X Y Z A B C D E F G H I J K L M N O P Q R S T
V W X Y Z A B C D E F G H I J K L M N O P Q R S T U
W X Y Z A B C D E F G H I J K L M N O P Q R S T U V
X Y Z A B C D E F G H I J K L M N O P Q R S T U V W
Y Z A B C D E F G H I J K L M N O P Q R S T U V W X
Z A B C D E F G H I J K L M N O P Q R S T U V W X Y
```

The cipher block sat on the table beside a letter whose words had all been scrambled into unreadable code.

"This came this morning," Bet said. "But just like all the rest, I couldn't read it."

She pressed her pen over the first letter of the code, which was *S*.

Beside the letter, it left a tiny dot.

Just like the ones Mary had seen on the Vigenère cipher, she realized with a shiver. Those dots must have been left when a Confederate coder used the cipher to decode other messages.

"I need to find the first letter of the key in the first column of the block," Bet said. She traced her pen down the first vertical column of the code block until she found the letter *M*, from *Manchester*.

"Then you go across the row until you find the coded letter," Mary said.

"Yes," Bet said. She moved her pen over to the *S* that appeared in the horizontal row.

"And then follow it up," Mary said.

Bet's pen began to move up the page.

"To the letter at the top of the column," Mary told her.

"That should be the original letter," Bet said, and noted it down: *G*.

The next letter they uncoded was *E*.

Then *N*.

Then *E* again.

"*General*," Mary said. "It spells *general*."

Bet looked at her, her eyes bright.

"You found it, Mary," she said. "You broke the code."

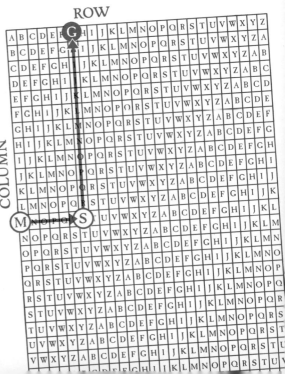

Mary didn't like something about the way the Davis house looked when she returned from the meeting with Bet.

She couldn't put her finger on it.

Maybe the backyard was a little too quiet.

Maybe the front porch was a little too deserted.

But her footsteps slowed as she came up the street.

And as she did, she noticed another woman who worked for the Davis family coming down it toward her.

"What's happening at the house?" Mary asked, as the two of them met.

"Where have you been?" the woman asked. Then she leaned in to tell Mary the news.

"They're going to H**A**N**G** the baker,"

she said.

"The baker?" Mary repeated. "McNiven?"

The woman nodded. "He's a spy," she said. "They've got police at the house. Want to talk to everyone."

With that, the woman took off again down the street.

Mary took another step toward the house, but then she hesitated.

As she did, a man in uniform came out onto the porch of the house. Mary was close enough now that they stood in clear view of each other.

But he hadn't noticed her. Not yet.

Then someone else came out onto the porch: O'Melia.

With a single swift glance, O'Melia scanned the entire street.

In an instant, her eyes fixed on Mary.

Mary couldn't hear what O'Melia said, but suddenly the man was staring at Mary, too.

Then he was shouldering his weapon and taking strides across the porch toward her.

Mary bolted.

She could hear the man shouting behind her, but that only made her run faster.

She turned down street after street and alley after alley, until she couldn't hear his footsteps any longer.

Then she slipped into a shed and hid under a blanket that had been thrown over a pile of wood.

And she didn't come out again until night fell.

———◇◇◇◇◇———

It was less than a dozen blocks, through familiar streets, to Bet Van Lew's home.

But by the time Mary arrived, she was shaking like a leaf.

There was no answer to her first knock on the door.

When she knocked again, the sound of her own knuckles thudding on the fine wood filled her heart with fear.

Was there ANYONE inside to hear her?

What if Bet was GONE?

What if Bet was being WATCHED?

What if Bet had been TAKEN,
just like Thomas McNiven?

What if the FOOTSTEPS Mary could
hear now beyond the door weren't Bet's at all,
but belonged to a Confederate operative?

Then the door cracked open, and a beam of warm light split the darkness.

"Mary! What are you doing here?" Bet whispered.

Then she threw the door open wide and welcomed her in.

"You deserve better than this," Bet said.

The night was still dark, but the stench of the wagon Bet had ordered brought from her farm that very same night was unmistakable.

It was filled with a giant load of manure.

"I'm sorry," Bet said. "But this is the only thing I can be sure the soldiers won't search."

"It's not the hardest thing I've done," Mary said. "At least I know it will be over soon."

"This whole war will be over soon," Bet said.

"Thanks, in no small part, to YOU."

The two women embraced.

Then Mary climbed up in the back of the wagon and lay down in her hiding place: a shallow box to protect her from the stinking load.

The driver covered the box with manure, so nobody would have any idea she was there.

Then Mary felt the wagon below her lurch into motion.

The next time she saw the light was hours and hours later, in Philadelphia.

She heard the sounds of a city around her and felt the wagon roll to a stop.

She could hear orders being given and running footsteps.

More than one person clambered into the back of the wagon, to shovel away the load that hid her.

Then the lid of her box was pulled away, and kind hands helped her to stand.

Strangers helped her down from the wagon.

Then they led her into the house of an old Quaker couple, where a large tub of hot water waited for her. Mary bathed, and ate a warm meal.

And for the first time in years, she slept as deep and as long as she wanted, in a real bed.

When she woke up, she found a simple new dress laid out for her on a chair.

As she picked it up, she thought about everything she had left behind at the Confederate White House. There wasn't one thing she missed—except for her diary. She had fled so quickly that she hadn't had time to retrieve it from its hiding place. All those memories and thoughts she had hidden there, the story of years of her life—would she ever see it again?

She dressed and went down the stairs, which ended at the front door.

But she didn't stop there.

She pulled the door open and stepped out into the winter sun, walking wherever she wanted to, a free woman.

Emru twxeed,

L lgr'u erqh fcykhlvy M iiu, hlhtpk mb wor nmdrfnts.

Noxtv cpc suwsv mp dlijc uw dh?

Wy xs suuqwh jv r wws xn khh osveme, xbitr khh zgsua fi hmt ryogwviolirb.

Rprp

Can you decipher Mary's letter to Bet Van Lew to find out where Mary hid her diary?

Biographical Information

Just a few months after Mary escaped the Confederate White House, the Union army surrounded the Confederate army at the Battle of Appomattox Court House.

Confederate General Lee surrendered to Union General Grant on April 9, 1865.

After four years of fighting, the Civil War finally came to an end.

And so did slavery in the United States.

Within two weeks of the end of the war, **Mary Bowser** had already started to teach hundreds of Richmond children who had been freed from slavery how to read. She later shared her story with audiences that probably included Harriet Beecher Stowe. Her marriage to Wilson does not seem to have survived the war. The only words of her own that have been preserved come from correspondence she wrote to the Georgia Freedmen's Bureau: "I felt that . . . it was my duty if possible to work where I am most needed."

As Richmond fell, **Jefferson Davis** tried to evade Union capture wearing his wife's shawl, but was too tall to be mistaken for a woman. He spent two years in prison before being released to become president of an insurance company and write his own memoirs. He died of bronchitis and malaria in 1889.

In her later years, **Varina Davis** penned a column for the *New York World*, and wrote that she believed the right side had won the war; she became friends with General Grant's widow, Julia; met Booker T. Washington; and passed away in New York City in 1906.

Mary O'Melia operated a boardinghouse in Baltimore after the war and died in 1907.

Thomas McNiven was arrested three times under suspicion of being a spy, but never hanged. He survived the war and lived until 1904 in Richmond.

Elizabeth (Bet) Van Lew was the first person to raise the United States flag in Richmond after it fell to Union forces. General Grant wrote to her that she had sent him "the most valuable information received from Richmond during the war." Her fortune depleted by gathering intelligence, she took a job as postmaster in Richmond, where she employed several African Americans on her staff. Ostracized by Richmond society, she was also denied a pension by the United States government and struggled financially until her death in 1900.

Historical Note

Mary Bowser was an effective spy because she was a person whom almost nobody thought much about: an African American woman at a time when African Americans weren't allowed to read, and women weren't allowed to vote.

Sadly, this means that very few details of Mary's life survive today. Records indicate her baptism and marriage dates, and the fact that she was educated in the North and served as a teacher in Liberia before returning to Richmond to marry Wilson Bowser.

The details of exactly what she did during the war have largely been erased. Even after the Civil War, tensions between former Confederates and Union sympathizers were high. So the Union destroyed many of their intelligence records to protect the identities of people like Mary who had aided the Union effort but still had to live after the war among people who had fought for the Confederacy.

Stories like Mary's leave us with a lot of questions, not just about her, but about how history is written, and who writes it. Few people realized how important Mary's life was at the time, so we don't have all the facts we might like in order to write her personal history. But the history of the entire war is incomplete if it doesn't include Mary.

So this book tells Mary's story based on the facts

that are available: about her, about the war, and about the people around her whose lives were better documented.

History does record that Jefferson Davis suffered great mental strain over the presence of a mole in the highest reaches of the Confederacy. And some details about Mary's wartime service survive in the diary of Bet Van Lew. The timeline of the war, Lee's visit to the Davis home, and the Davis family travels are all accurate. And so is the timing of Mary's arrival at the Confederate White House, her first meeting with Bet at the dress shop, the signals they used to communicate, her relationship with her fellow spy Thomas McNiven, and her escape just before the end of the war.

After the war, Mary worked as a teacher. Some newspaper reports seem to indicate that she also told the story of her service as a spy to several audiences, including one that may have included Harriet Beecher Stowe.

Other evidence suggests that Mary may have remarried and moved to the Caribbean.

After her late twenties, the historical record for Mary Bowser runs out.

But by then, she'd already done more to change the course of history than many people do in a lifetime.

Bibliography

Abbott, Karen. *Liar, Temptress, Soldier, Spy: Four Women Undercover in the Civil War*. New York: HarperCollins, 2014.

Cashin, Joan E. *First Lady of the Confederacy: Varina Davis's Civil War*. Cambridge: Belknap Press, 2009.

Cooper, William J., Jr. *Jefferson Davis, American*. New York: Vintage, 2001.

Leveen, Lois. *The Secrets of Mary Bowser*. New York: William Morrow, 2012.

Van Lew, Elizabeth. *A Yankee Spy in Richmond: The Civil War Diary of "Crazy Bet" Van Lew*. Edited by David D. Ryan. Mechanicsburg, PA: Stackpole Books, 1996.

Varon, Elizabeth R. *Southern Lady, Yankee Spy: The True Story of Elizabeth Van Lew, a Union Agent in the Heart of the Confederacy*. New York: Oxford University Press, 2003.

WAIT!
Have you solved Mary's last mystery?

Don't crack this seal until you've cracked the code!

Answer Key

Copyright page: The black letters spell out "Clues are all around but beware false flowers lie."

Page 10: The map of the house and garden is used as a reference for many other clues. By process of elimination, you can narrow down where the diary might be hiding. Many other pages hint that you should return to page 10 to help with your search.

Page 13: If you place the red acetate over the picture frame, it says, "Vigenère Loves This Picture." The image is of a bird of paradise (the bird) in a cage, surrounded by birds-of-paradise (the flowers).

Page 16: Place the red acetate over the top of the image to reveal "COMMUNICATION PROTOCOL A=M SHIFT CIPHER." View the rest of the page through the acetate to remove the red letters, then translate the black letters with the Caesar cipher wheel (found in spy envelope) set at A=M. The book page on the left says, "The diary is not in the nursery," while the book page on the right says, "It is not in the library."

Page 21: Use the white vellum with the rectangular cutouts (included in the spy envelope) to decode this clue. With the Caesar cipher set at M=B, decode the letters at the bottom of the vellum to read "Put me over the flower that tells the truth." Then on page 21, if you line up the corner art on the vellum with the white chrysanthemums (which mean "truth" in the language of flowers) in place of the page number on page 21, the cutouts reveal: "the code used to translate into English is bird of paradise."

Page 23: The language of flowers is used many other times in the book to give hints or red herrings. Snapdragons, which symbolize deception in the language of flowers, are used as borders on pages with false clues. Along the sides of the paper are the words "listen to O'Melia" written in Morse code. In the story, she talks about Mrs. Davis's favorite flower, the bird-of-paradise, which is the key to the Vigenère cipher at the end of the book.

Pages 24 and 25: Pictures of rhododendrons used in place of page numbers hint that Mary buried her diary under this type of flower in the garden.

Page 28: The Morse code key on the desk is here to help decode the various clues throughout the book.

Page 31: The border on this page is made of snapdragons, which mean "deception." With the cipher set to M=B, the decoded text reads, "The diary is in the Davis bedroom."

Page 33: A building in the right upper corner shows the cipher key U=H. With the Caesar cipher set to U=H, the border frame reveals the phrase "use the map to find the diary." The number 10 or X is hidden ten times in this image so you realize the "map" they are talking about is the house map on page 10. Signs all across town spell out "find a three word phrase without spaces," hinting at "birdofparadise."

Page 40: The music notes on this page spell out the word *CAGE* twice, providing a hint to look at the one image of a cage in the book: the bird of paradise in a cage on page 13. If you use the red acetate over the red dresses, you can see the words "Not in dining room." There are ten women wearing red, again linking back to the map on page 10.

Page 45: The Morse code reads, "Check the icebox," but it's on the page with a snapdragon border, meaning the clue is false.

Page 47: The picture of rhododendrons in the bottom right-hand corner provides a hint that the diary is buried under them.

Page 50: With the Caesar cipher set to M=B, the text on the side of the desk says, "Not in here." The panels on the door in the hallway reflect the room layout of the White House as illustrated on page 10. The door has the number 10 above it. An X over certain panels on the door suggests the diary is not in the corresponding rooms. The rooms indicated are: O'Melia's room, the nursery, and the foyer.

Page 52: If you hold the sides of the page directly against a flat mirror, the reflection finishes the other half of the letters and tells you where to line up your cipher for the next clue: MB=CODE. When decoded, the text on the page reads "Page ~ Line ~ Word," a hint for how to solve the *Uncle Tom's Cabin* excerpt (included in the spy envelope) clue.

Page 53: Ten birds are flying in the sky. The number 10 also appears on the side of the carriage, connecting back to the map on page 10. "No" is written in Morse code beneath and above windows in answer to the unspoken question "Is the diary in this room?" On the ground the lines in the dirt form the words "It is outside." The side of the carriage says "Not all birds fly," which hints to the bird-of-paradise flower.

Page 57: The cipher image is set to M=B. The paper in Mary's hand decodes to "Beware of dragons," a reminder not to trust clues on pages with snapdragons, and the paper to the right says, "Think on Mrs. Davis's favorite."

Page 62: As on page 52, if you hold this page up to a mirror, the cut-off border letters spell out "Icebox = Hoax," reinforcing that the clue on page 45 is false.

Page 63: The note on the nightstand says, "Use the Mirror." If you look closely at the wallpaper using your mirror, you can see the words "NOT IN HERE." The page border frame has the words "find mary's diary," also in mirrored lettering. The bottom part of the frame has the words "find the key phrase" in mirrored text.

Page 65: The wheel has the words "Mary's initials unlock a key" hidden on it. Use the Caesar cipher set to M=B to decode the text on the back edge of the cart: "not in the larder." The bakery name, seen in reverse on the cart's cover, is Paradise Bakery, which again links to the final code-breaking phrase, "birdofparadise."

Page 69: The Morse code along the frame of Mary and Bet reading a letter translates to "line up the curtains at the wheel." The curtains in the main illustration have the letters *M* and *B* in their folds, so with the cipher set to M=B, the decoded text along the baseboard reads "dig for the diary." Words in the wallpaper at the upper-right corner of the main illustration say, "not in here."

Page 72: The number 10 written on the building refers back to the map on page 10. The cipher letters O and Z on the back of the cart shows another part of the cipher set to the M=B position, this time focusing on the Z=O. The frame says "not in the laundry" in Morse code on the top and "not in the kitchen" in Morse code on the bottom. If you put the red acetate over the wood grain on the door, you see the words "search for the diary."

Uncle Tom's Cabin excerpt (included in spy envelope): Throughout the book, readers will find mysterious numbers in the formation 63 ~ 8 ~ 4. The numbers change, but the formation, with the ~ symbol, is consistent. But on page 52, they see this: EPVT ~ AXCT ~ LDGS

If the cipher wheel is set to M=B, the code spells out: Page ~ Line ~ Word.

A hint for the cipher code is present on page 57, where the image of the cipher is lined up at M=B, and the letters *M* and *B* appear on the background buildings. If you use the page from *Uncle Tom's Cabin* (which is an excerpt from page 63 of Harriet Beecher Stowe's novel) and follow the formula so that the first number is always the page, the second is the line on the page, and the third is the word, then you find the following:

63 ~ 8 ~ 4 (page 27)   63 ~ 20 ~ 3 (page 56)
63 ~ 12 ~ 1 (page 51)   63 ~ 24 ~ 3 (page 67)
63 ~ 14 ~ 4 (page 39)   63 ~ 25 ~ 3 (page 18)
63 ~ 16 ~ 3 (page 47)   63 ~ 29 ~ 2 (page 42)
63 ~ 19 ~ 3 (page 32)   63 ~ 29 ~ 3 (page 15)

Together the words say: "Plant it in the garden and see it fly away." This is a riddle. The answer, of course, is bird-of-paradise.

Page 79: Mary's letter is decoded using "birdofparadise" as the key for the Vigenère cipher...

Dear friend,

I don't want anything I had, except
my own memories.

Would you bring my diary to me?

It is buried in a tin in the garden,
under the roots of the rhododendron.

Mary